THE MYSTERY OF THE SEVENTEEN PILOT FISH

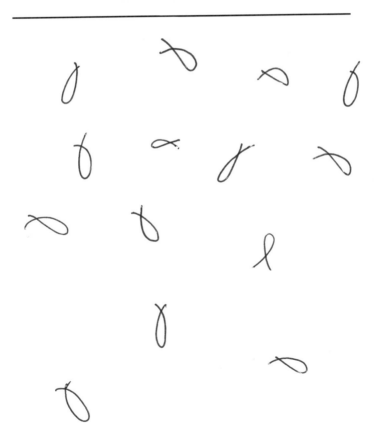

The Mystery of the Seventeen Pilot Fish
© 2016 Mike Kleine

Published by Plays Inverse Press
New York, NY
www.playsinverse.com

ISBN 13: 978-0-9914183-4-3

First Printing: August 2016
Cover design by Austin Breed
Page design by Tyler Crumrine
Printed in the U.S.A.

PLAYS
INVERSE

...trans-dimensional chem trails ... Dracula never died... island drops...

THE MYSTERY OF THE SEVENTEEN PILOT FISH

MIKE KLEINE

for Unity

...observing the purple abyss...

— Michael

January 10, 2021

...slurp the atmosphere...

...synth choir chant sounds coming from the mountains...

PLAYS INVERSE PRESS
NEW YORK, NY
2016

...trans-dimensional /
from the
mountains...

To Christian "X-Man" Caminiti

The Emperor Suan Sung asked the painter Li Chin Chi to paint the screens of his bedroom. The painter drew a landscape of mountains and waterfalls. A few days later the Emperor complained: "Your waterfalls make too much noise. I can no longer sleep."

Raúl Ruiz, Poetics of Cinema (Editions Dis Voir)

Today I feel electric grey / I hope tomorrow neon black.

Andre 3000, Interlude

The man opens the door to a house and walks in. The house is simple but well-designed. It consists of a single room, and in the middle of the room there is a couch and not much of anything else. The floor is painted blue, made to look like the ocean, and it is covered in fish, and the fish all look very sad. There is: an angler, a bat ray, some betta fish, a hog sucker, a chimaera, two blue sharks, a stone loach, a snook, three mahi-mahi, six herring, two ladyfish, a grouper, nine permits, a barracuda, a snapper, salmon, scamp, pinfish, two croakers, five bank seabass, a menhaden, jumping mullet, a searobin, spadefish, little tunny, a varden, halibut, hāpuku, mackerel, kahawai, two warehou, three crappies, a bass, yellow perch, five tarpon, a zander, two seven-figure pygmy goby, a redfish, an orange roughy, nine barreleye, a few cobias, a sailfish, swordfish, a Mexican golden trout, several shortfin mako, a flashlight fish, a two stripe damselfish, a Modoc sucker, five hickory shad, a pompano, two flounder, eight grey triggerfish, a knobbed porgy, an alligator, a Chinese algae eater, a blind cave fish, a megalodon, Nile tilapia, a kaluga, six agatha, a mandarinfish, two wahoo, a basking shark, seventy-three doctor fish, a giant trevally, European plaice, a Japanese amberjack, tambaqui, Arctic grayling, steelhead, eight stingray, three oscar fish, a Death Valley pupfish, a spot, three seahorses, half a rice eel, a silver arowana, a goldfish, a ram cichlid, common carp, paracanthurus hepatus, a worm eel, a zebra fish, twenty-seven koi, an Atlantic tarpon, a green sturgeon, an ocean sunfish, a cookiecutter shark, zander, five candiru, an Atlantic mackerel, pterophyllum scalare, two beluga, argyrosomus regius, a flathead grey mullet, a basa fish, a doctor fish, twelve anchovies, a vampire fish and, scattered about the room in various places, seventeen pilot fish. The rest of the house is pretty much empty. There is also a woman and a man wearing a bathrobe.

MAN: May I sit?

The man wearing a bathrobe stands off to one corner of the room. The song "Watermelon in Easter Hay" by Frank Zappa is playing from somewhere in the sky.

MAN IN BATHROBE: You may sit.

The man sits.

MAN: I am sitting.

The woman takes her time and walks over and shuts the door to the front of the house and walks back toward the couch. She is careful not to step on any of the fish. The couch where the man is sitting is in the middle of the ocean and when something is in the middle of the ocean, it floats very slowly. She says this to herself multiple times.

WOMAN: *[to herself]* ...when something is in the middle of the ocean, it floats very slowly.

MAN: *[sitting on the couch]* The couch is not floating. *[flicking some dry paint off the cuff of his Drôle de Monsieur jacket]* And this is not an ocean, *[pointing to the hāpuku on the floor]* this is just blue paint on a hardwood floor.

The woman keeps walking toward the couch, even more slowly, still repeating her mantra.

MAN IN BATHROBE: *[to the man sitting on the couch]* If that couch is not in the middle of the ocean, then this woman is not my wife.

The woman eventually reaches the couch. She sits down with a sigh.

WOMAN: *[sigh]*

MAN IN BATHROBE: *[still to the man sitting on the couch]* I am the husband.

In Andalusia, Pyramid Man kills himself and the man they call Gideon points to a circle in the sky and says a few words. The circle transforms into something yellow and the two men disappear, forever.

MAN: No you're not. You're not the husband. And this, again, *[pointing to the floor]* is not an ocean. I'm sorry but *[now disappointed]* I'm just not impressed by any of this.

Nearby, Godzilla happens and people die like they did at Lake Mercury.

MAN IN BATHROBE: *[in a deadpan sort of way]* I am not trying to impress you.

MAN: Yes, you are.

WOMAN: *[to the man]* We are not trying to impress you.

The man closes his eyes and blinks pictures of pyramids—a world of pyramids, everywhere. A world where a performance artist does a show behind a ranch house and transforms into a pyramid and floats up into the sky, disappearing, forever.

MAN IN BATHROBE: *[pointing to the woman sitting on the couch]* Do not say anything. And you are not my wife.

MAN: *[looking at the woman sitting on the couch]* Yes, she is.

After 100 million years, the men arrive at Mega Fortress 9 and the sky is a sherbet orange.

MAN IN BATHROBE: *[pause] [to the man]* My half sister.

WOMAN: *[interrupting the argument between the*

man and the man in the bathrobe] There is something
in our walls and it just won't leave.

*The sun goes down and the man with the mask stands
in the shadow of the house. Something in the wall makes
a sound. The man is now afraid. And the sky is pourpré.*

MAN: *[jumps a little, and then, to the woman]* Do
you have any idea what it could be?

*Somewhere else, four men—Garcìa, Bolaño, Saramago
and Márquez—ride through the desert at night. It's hot
instead of cold. A wormhole appears. Garcìa, who claims
to have dealt with this kind of thing in the past, speaks
to the entity and his voice comes back garbled: a foreign
tongue. Garcìa fires a round at the cosmic manifestation
but this does nothing. Eventually, the hole swallows
Saramago and the rest of the men flee.*

MAN IN BATHROBE: *[pointing to the wall]* We
think it's a woman.

MAN: Okay. *[pause]* What kind of woman?

*Something in the wall makes a sound [again]. The Hell
Priest appears, somewhere in the desert, one last time
again.*

MAN: *[to the man in the bathrobe]* What if it's a man?

WOMAN: Je suis devenu un magicien noir.

The desert is endless. Scorpions evaporate and become one with the air. The house in the middle of the desert is not a house but a vessel. There is a totem outside, near the house, made of sticks and wood and mud and tears and flesh. The woman outside, she tells the explorers, "They took him to a place in Algiers because he refused to fight." They drink the coffee and eat the meal made of figs and dates and raisins. They bash her head on a rock. One of the explorers says to the other explorer (the one who bashed the head of the woman onto the rock) "Why did you do such a thing?" The explorer responsible for committing the violent crime, the one with the asthma, traps an insect in one of the coffee tins and stuffs it into his pack. There is silence, and then, finally, "Because I have forgotten what it feels like to mean."

MAN IN BATHROBE: *[looking at the woman]* No. *[talking to the man]* We actually think it might be some sort of mythical creature. Something from the classics. *[to the wall]* Why don't you figure it out?

The man is now confused by the man in the bathrobe so he repeats the phrase to himself.

MAN: *[to himself]* Some sort of mythical creature. From the classics.

MAN IN BATHROBE: No, a mythical creature. *[pointing to the wall]* In our walls.

*Things shift and move and there is a slight earthquake.
Planet Earth morphs and disappears—then reappears as
a cube from the 9th dimension.*

MAN: *[looking at the wall off to the left of the couch,
where the sound came from]* I know. But what if it's
just a rodent or, you know, a bird? Something.

MAN IN BATHROBE: Can't be.

*The Master of the Universe decides he has had enough
and is done playing house. He leaves to go on vacation,
forever, and never returns.*

MAN: And why not?

MAN IN BATHROBE: *[to the woman in a rather
proud voice]* We don't keep pets.

WOMAN: *[quietly snickers]*

MAN IN BATHROBE: *[to the man]* So no, it could
not be a rodent.

MAN: Okay, so maybe it's a squirrel.

The wall makes another sound. Monsters from outer

space attack a ruined city nearby: Adelaide.

WOMAN: It's not a squirrel.

MAN IN BATHROBE: You're the detective. You tell us.

Znhwcnbbnwe materializes. Pyramid detectives walk through the desert landscape—now filled with superheroes and aliens and cowboys and dried-up dog shit.

MAN: *[to the man in the bathrobe]* I'm the detective?

MAN IN BATHROBE: *[nodding his head up and down]* A true detective. *[smacking his lips]* I said, this is a mystery. We don't know what's going on. I don't know how to solve mysteries. You're the *true* detective.

MAN: True detective?

Monsters appear in the middle of the desert from out of the sand.

MAN IN BATHROBE: True detective. *[pointing to the fish on the ground]* There's fish everywhere.

WOMAN: *[pause]* So who's the bad guy?

DETECTIVE: What?

MAN IN BATHROBE: If we have a detective, *[pointing to the detective]* then we also need a bad guy. *[pointing to the woman]* Isn't that how these things work?

DETECTIVE: What things?

MAN IN BATHROBE: These mysteries?

DETECTIVE: Mysteries? *[pause]* I'm not sure. This is my first mystery.

God returns and changes his name to Michael, the Creator—but it is too late.

MAN IN BATHROBE: *[to the detective, now with his eyebrows raised a little]* Only your first time?

DETECTIVE: My first time. Yes. *[pause]* I'm not that old. *[pause]* Quite young actually.

MAN IN BATHROBE: *[to the woman]* Young.

WOMAN: Pfft. Young.

There is a very awkward silence that lasts seventeen seconds. Then "Give Me A Love" by Jimmy Riley rumbles from somewhere beneath the ground, muffled.

MAN IN BATHROBE: *[in an interrupting sort of voice]* Very well then—let's fix this problem.

DETECTIVE: *[with his arms out]* That's what I'm here to do.

MAN IN BATHROBE: *[to the detective]* Ah. Good then. You're the detective?

DETECTIVE: I'm the detective.

The detective and the man in the bathrobe have a quick staring contest. It lasts seventeen seconds. The man in the bathrobe loses because he blinks. In Adelaide, the night quickly becomes a shiny darkness made of ochre and moonlight and the city becomes even more ruined.

DETECTIVE: *[hands in the air]* I win.

MAN IN BATHROBE: Look here, *[pointing to the woman]* we both pay our taxes on time and live in this house. It's not rented. This is my house. *[to the* *woman]* I paid for all of this so, you're the bad guy.

The wall makes the sound of a bad guy.

BAD GUY: *[raising her hand]* Fine! I'm the bad guy and this *[pointing to the zebra fish on the ground]* is our house.

DETECTIVE: *[to the bad guy]* No one's the bad guy here.

MAN IN BATHROBE: That Mexican golden trout is not our—my house.

BAD GUY: Okay, so I'm the bad guy woman, whatever. This is still my house. And that *[pointing to the zebra fish]* is not a Mexican golden trout.

Offstage, the man in the golden mask commands a lamp to destroy the history of the earth and the universe. A servant serves minestrone soup in a chilled bowl made of nothing.

DETECTIVE: *[to the man in the bathrobe]* It's a zebra fish. *[pause]* Now, please, enough with all this nonsense.

MAN IN BATHROBE: What nonsense? *[shrugging]*

This is our house. We can do as we please in our own house.

DETECTIVE: No, I mean, yes—of course you can—but please, stop with the good guy/bad guy thing.

MAN IN BATHROBE: *[smiling]* Okay fine, I suppose. *[smiling even harder]* But this is our house.

DETECTIVE: How about this—you are both time travelers and you do home invasions?

BAD GUY WOMAN: This is our house. And no, we do not do home invasions.

The man in the golden mask swims to the minuscule island nation of Fjjjjjcrqusccs. The trip itself turns out to be rather dull, stressful and supremely uneventful. And it isn't until his eventual arrival that he happens upon hundreds and thousands of cosmic wormholes and corpses—dozens upon dozens of cadavres of men of all shapes and sizes and color—strewn about, across the entirety of the vast but infinitesimally small mini-island, with the stink of volcano in the air. Also, on the beach by the rocks and seaweed: the remains of what appears to have been some sort of titanic chemical aeroplane and the aftermath of some gigantic firefight, with men wearing balaclavas and designer clothes—also, the body of a green monster from another world. But mainly, men in masks and very expensive clothing.

MAN IN BATHROBE: *[picks up Satanic Bible and opens to a random verse]* We once traveled to the house on the hill, *[points to the window]* you know, the one where you can go to speak with God? *[pauses]* Anyway, we went there but He was not there. There is a mineral they are looking for *[pointing to the window]*—they have been looking for it for centuries—and our planet has this mineral. They need this mineral, obviously. And these things, they will do whatever it takes to get this mineral. I don't know. It's something we cannot see. It goes beyond the electromagnetic spectrum. But you *[pointing to the bad guy woman]* are the bad guy woman and this is what it's like after the end of the world has already happened.

DETECTIVE: *[takes out his Moleskine and begins scribbling]* This is good. *[more scribbling]* You guys are like that lovable sociopath, Ruis López.

MAN IN BATHROBE: You know, for a detective, you're not very smart. *[drops Satanic Bible]* *[his hangnail pulses]*

The centaur pauses to stare at her reflection in the lake and the centaur thinks, for a fleeting moment, Who is this person?

DETECTIVE: No, I'm not. *[pointing the cap end of his fountain pen at the man in the bathrobe]* As I pointed out before, I'm very literally quite young. *[pause]* And inexperienced.

The wall makes the sound of buttered waffles slamming against hard pavement on a hot summer day. A cactus in the Cactus Room explodes and there is the sound of women crying. Blood and rotting meat. The cactus exploding is filled with visions of dead ancestors.

BAD GUY WOMAN: *[putting her hand down after yawning]* *[to the detective]* Okay now you're just being an asshole.

DETECTIVE: *[stops writing and turns to the bad guy woman]* Are you speaking to your husband?

BAD GUY WOMAN: The man in the bathrobe, *[points at the man in the bathrobe]* he won't leave my house. He's not my husband. He's definitely the bad guy. *[pause]* I also think he might be holding me hostage. *[to the room]* This is a home invasion. This is my house. And time travel is a broken thing.

DETECTIVE: *[squinting a little at the man in the bathrobe]* So this is a home invasion house?

A man in a wet Tom Ford black slim-fit peak lapel wool suit shoots a tennis shoe commercial for Nike in the middle of the desert, with lights and cameras and tents and trailers and vans and buses and girls everywhere. There's a Mickey Mouse too—somewhere.

BAD GUY WOMAN: *[to the detective]* I don't think

I know what that is.

DETECTIVE: Well, for starters, do you really believe this man *[pointing to the man in the bathrobe]* is holding—*[pause]* holding you hostage *[to the bad guy woman]* in your own home?

The bad guy woman nods.

DETECTIVE: *[to the man in the bathrobe]* Are you holding her hostage? *[to the bad guy woman]* Also, *[quickly]* I don't mean to be an asshole. *[looks back at the man in the bathrobe]*

BAD GUY WOMAN: *[to the detective]* Asshole.

MAN IN BATHROBE: *[hand on chest]* Am I holding her hostage?

The architect in the house across the street watches the man, bad guy woman and man in the bathrobe on an old VHS tape from 1998. He says, "The world is a simulation and we are the only ones ruining it." He smiles.

DETECTIVE: Yes, that's what I just said—asked of you. Are you holding her hostage?

MAN IN BATHROBE: *[in a declarative sort of voice]*

I am not holding *[points to the bad guy woman]* this woman hostage. This is my house. *[to the wall]* This is not a home invasion house. *[screaming]* *[getting red in the face]* THIS IS MY *[spittle everywhere]* *[snot begins to run]* HOUSE! *[pause]* And time travel is not real—it does not exist.

BAD GUY WOMAN: *[getting red in the face]* It is not and *[yelling]* YOU ARE HOLDING ME HOSTAGE HERE IN MY OWN HOME.

At this point time freezes. The television plays the news and Michael Jordan is talking to a woman reporter about his new shoe. Michael Jordan says, "This is the Air Jordan and it is my shoe. It is a new shoe." He holds up the shoe and the camera zooms in on the shoe. "It was designed by Peter Moore and it has red and black accents. See, look." Michael Jordan points at the red and black accents on the shoe. "Remember that name: Peter Moore," Michael Jordan says. "I like Peter Moore because Peter Moore gets what I'm about. He understands what it means to be Michael Jordan. I am going to wear Peter Moore shoes until the day I die." The woman reporter says, "That is wonderful—fantastic news, Michael Jordan. These are some great shoes. My son, I'm sure, would love a pair." "I will wear these shoes at my basketball games and then I will wear the same shoes, but a different pair, when I am outside and not playing my basketball games." "Impressive." There isn't even a moment for silence or for anything but what is happening. "Peter Moore is making more shoes. He told me last week at a weekend party somewhere near the beach. I think he is making other shoes in different colors. I am not sure, but I will ask him next time I see him—Peter Moore." Michael Jordan looks into the camera. The woman reporter says some words and asks Michael Jordan a seemingly vague question about the youth and contemporary society—how he feels about everything. "I am going to be wearing Air Jordans everywhere I go from now on. Air Jordans are me and if you don't believe me, they are going to become me. I believe Air Jordans are the future of basketball." Michael Jordan says something else about the design of the shoe and how, because of this, it is a much better shoe than any other shoe available right now. Time unfreezes.

MAN IN BATHROBE: This woman [still pointing to the bad guy woman with the red face sitting on the couch next to the detective who is also sitting on the couch] is my wife, [to the detective] good sir, and I am not holding my own wife [slaps his hand against his own face] hostage. Unless you consider marriage some sort of hostage situation.

DETECTIVE: [to the bad guy woman] [earnestly] Is he holding you hostage? I'm asking because I'm not sure.

BAD GUY WOMAN: [nodding her head up and down vigorously] Yes, I'm quite sure he is. [pause] And stop being an asshole!

The man in the bathrobe quickly puts his hands down and suddenly, he's sitting on the floor, cross-legged. For some reason, he is also grinning.

MAN IN BATHROBE: *[to the detective]* Okay Dick, let's play a game. *[still grinning]*

DICK: *[to the man in the bathrobe]* My name's not Dick.

The bad guy woman does the motion of a hand job in the air.

MAN IN BATHROBE: I watch a lot of films.

DICK: *[no answer]*

MAN IN BATHROBE: Okay. *[pause]* So your name's not Dick.

DETECTIVE: Okay. Good.

MAN IN BATHROBE: So, in my left hand, I have two beans. One bean, the grey one, this one, *[showing the grey bean to the detective]* wins. The other bean, the black one, *[showing the black bean to the detective]* doesn't.

BAD GUY WOMAN: *[rolling her eyes]* Not this shit again.

A man successfully summons a daemon from Ar'Kenon 9, and for the next 500 years evades death as an immortal.

DETECTIVE: *[intrigued like a child would be]* Okay. *[scooting up onto the edge of the couch where the man in the bathrobe is orchestrating the game]* Let's play.

MAN IN BATHROBE: The winning bean, *[flicking the grey bean into the air]* which in this case is the grey one, *[the bean lands back into his right hand]* will be in this hand. The black bean *[flicking the black bean into the air]* will be *[the bean lands back into his left hand]* in this hand. Choose wisely. *[pause]* If you pick the black bean, all bets are off. *[the man in the bathrobe puts both hands behind his back]* If you win, I will tell you whether I'm holding this woman hostage or not.

BAD GUY WOMAN: *[silence]*

DETECTIVE: And if I lose?

MAN IN BATHROBE: Then I will tell you whether I'm holding this woman hostage or not and what those noises coming from the wall really mean.

DETECTIVE: The noises coming from the wall?

MAN IN BATHROBE: [nods to the wall] I'll tell you what they mean.

The man/detective suddenly realizes that the man in the bathrobe is quite clever and, most likely, the woman's husband. But at the same time, the man/detective also realizes that there is no way he will be able to prove this to anyone unless he plays the man in the bathrobe's game with the beans. If the winning bean is truly in the right hand of the man in the bathrobe—who is also a liar and, most likely, the husband of the woman—then he will lie about the bean being in his right hand and the man/detective will be forced to find out about the noises coming from the wall. But then again, if the man in the bathrobe is actually telling the truth—and still, really the husband of the woman—then the bean will really be in his right hand and the man/detective will once and for all find out whether the man in the bathrobe is really holding the woman hostage.

DETECTIVE: [to the man in the bathrobe] [to the bad guy woman] I love you guys.

The wall makes the sound of chains and feet and an American poet decides it is necessary to compose a poem about the end of the world and the universe. The poet dedicates the poem to a McDonald's and a picture of some trees somewhere in Delaware.

MAN IN BATHROBE: So which hand will it be?

DETECTIVE: This is the best day of my life.

An aeroplane falls from out of the sky.

BAD GUY WOMAN: *[to the man]* You can call me Heather.

No one survives.

MAN IN BATHROBE: *[to Heather]* He may not!

Now, people are having a loud conversation outside Heather/the bad guy woman's house. Daft Punk is playing. A man looks up into the night sky and prays. Just over the horizon, flashes of light—an aeroplane falls from out of the sky, again, and a prophet speaks of deception and men in the clouds: the daemons of Ar'Kenon 9. A woman says, "Kunta." Palm trees and expensive cars. Four air conditioning units and smoke on everything.

DETECTIVE: *[to the bad guy woman, all giddy]* Heather, which one shall I pick?

BAD GUY WOMAN: My name's not Heather. *[to the people having a loud conversation outside her house]* Why are you guys being such assholes? *[in an even louder voice]* I am being held hostage by two men here. One of them is a detective. Please *[pause]* help! *[assertively]* This is my house and I think I need to get out.

DETECTIVE: *[silence]*

Offstage, a slave says to another slave, "Cancel the end of the world—not today." The other slave, he realizes, I don't know how to do that.

BAD GUY WOMAN: I'm calling the police. *[pause] [looks at the detective]* And I mean the *real* police.

DETECTIVE: *[rubbing his hands together and smiling]* Oh hush about all that, *[shushing the bad guy woman]* I'm not holding you hostage. *[pointing to the man wearing the bathrobe who is most likely her husband]* He is. I'm also here to solve a mystery. I am the real police. I am the end of the world. *[sounding real happy now]* My oh my, how this is quickly becoming a very exciting game!

BAD GUY WOMAN: *[to the detective]* I mean it. I will call the police.

MAN IN BATHROBE: *[to the detective]* She means it.

DETECTIVE: *[to the man in the bathrobe and the bad guy woman]* Okay.

At this point, the man has failed as a detective and can no longer go on as a detective. The detective, again, becomes just a man. An aeroplane falls from out of the sky, and the man happens to notice this just as it is happening, as if for the very first time. He looks out the windows and also realizes the sun is now setting. He looks at the palm trees in the distance and imagines everything in a state of constant melting. He hears a sizzling in the wind and sees the same red cars you see in movies driven by men that do not look like men, and it is too much.

MAN: *[touching himself]* Now I am relaxed.

MAN IN BATHROBE: *[looking into the man's eyes]* I've only ever told the truth twice. This is one of those times.

MAN: *[still touching himself and grinning wildly]* So this is three times?

One of the people having a loud conversation outside the bad guy woman's house mentions something about doing Jell-O shots off his adopted sister's body.

MAN IN BATHROBE: *[nodding his head toward the bad guy woman]* This woman is my life.

BAD GUY WOMAN: *[to the man sitting on the couch]* Don't believe him!

The man thinks to himself.

MAN: *[to the bad guy woman]* Are you his wife?

MAN IN BATHROBE: *[to the man]* Ask me another question.

MAN: *[addressing the man in the bathrobe]* Are those people outside, who are being very loud, *[pointing to the wall]* friends of yours?

Another one of the people having a loud conversation outside the bad guy woman's house asks the guy to be more specific about doing Jell-O shots off his adopted sister's body. There is a laughter that is not nervous.

MAN IN BATHROBE: If you leave this house right now and go back to where you came from *[he points to the door the man entered at the beginning]*, I promise you, you will find the answer to your question.

MAN: Which question?

MAN IN BATHROBE: The question you just asked.

MAN: The one about the people outside?

Two samurai in a wheat field slice at each other. There doesn't appear to be any cuts but they cut into each other, again and again and again. Nothing at first, just silence. But then geysers of the stuff—red water everywhere. Jet streams in the sky and microtels nearby. Then nothing, again. Vapour trails. They fall to the ground.

MAN IN BATHROBE: *[pause]* The one about whether or not I'm the husband.

MAN: No, I want to know about the people outside. Like, who are they really? Could they be daemons? Or maybe even ghosts? *[he makes ghost sounds with his mouth] [pause]* No, they're probably really just a bunch of assholes. Old friends from college, huh?

BAD GUY WOMAN: I know them enough to know that they always do this. *[to the man]* They're not really assholes and he *[pointing to the man in the bathrobe]* knows them! They are his accomplices— they are going to press the reset button.

One of the assholes outside says, "221 days and five hours and three minutes." The song "dlp 1.1" by William Basinski plays from someone's brand-new car stereo.

MAN: *[to the man in the bathrobe]* So, she just answered my question. I don't really need to leave anymore now do I?

MAN IN BATHROBE: But how can you be so sure it's the truth? Maybe she's lying.

One of the people outside, the one who mentioned something about doing Jell-O shots off his adopted sister's body, says, "Stomach," as another kid goes into the alley and, by accident, discovers the totem made of wood, metal and meat.

MAN: Okay, I choose the door.

The bad guy woman tries to get up to stop the man from leaving but the man in the bathrobe tells her to sit down.

MAN IN BATHROBE: *[to the bad guy woman]* Sit down!

The bad guy woman sits.

MAN: *[looking at the bad guy woman and feeling sorry for her life]* Okay, I change my mind. *[again, to the man in the bathrobe and pointing to the door]* I'm staying. *[pause]* Because I want to save you. *[he points at the bad guy woman]* So these are friends of yours? *[motioning to the wall but really trying to point at outside, where the people are talking and being very loud]*

MAN IN BATHROBE: *[silence]* *[he looks at both of*

his hands, each holding a bean, and waits]

MAN: *[clears his throat and then looks at the bad guy woman]* Is this real? *[to the bad guy woman]* Tell me this is for real.

The people having a loud conversation outside the bad guy woman's house all begin to laugh very loudly about something. Vibrations and critter thoughts become whole again. The wall.

BAD GUY WOMAN: *[very slowly]* This is for real.

The man in the bathrobe begins to cough violently and uncontrollably. Blood spatters the back of his hand. There is also a piece of tissue paper. He drops the beans and begins to roll around on the ground. Some men fly out to an oilrig in the middle of the Pacific because they want to try and stop that which cannot be stopped. Someone in Saskatchewan asks the question, "Will they survive?"

BAD GUY WOMAN: Not the fish!

He rolls onto several of the fish.

MAN: *[standing up from the couch and talking to the man in the bathrobe rolling on the floor, coughing uncontrollably]* So what happens now?

The man in the bathrobe continues to cough. He can't hear the man talking to him. The man in the bathrobe's face is quickly becoming red.

MAN: No! Don't die now. *[pause]* Die later. Is this really where I'm at right now? A house where a man wearing a bathrobe tells me to play games and then decides to die?

BAD GUY WOMAN: *[to the man]* I'm not his wife.

The ghost of Superman walks through the bad guy woman but no one notices.

BAD GUY WOMAN: *[shivers]*

MAN: This is <u>so</u> not fair! *[points at the camera offstage]* I'm getting the cameras.

The man tries to grab a camera from one of the stagehands offstage. The understudy is excited.

DIRECTOR OF PLAY: *[waving a rolled up script at the man]* Go back onto the stage. Now!

The man returns to the stage and opens the mouth of the man in the bathrobe to see if there is a hidden camera inside his body but the bad guy woman stands and grabs the man by the shoulder and left arm before he can open the mouth of the man in the bathrobe completely. The man is too strong for the bad guy woman so she lets go and the man walks over to the man in the bathrobe and his lips are now beginning to turn blue. He is gagging. The man opens the man in the bathrobe's mouth. It stinks of poultry. He continues to choke on something and a few moments later, a yellow canary flies out. Surprised, the man staggers backward and steps onto a fish. He looks down and sees it's the hog sucker. The man in the bathrobe is still choking.

MAN: Oh, not the hog sucker. *[fish guts cling to the bottom of his shoe]*

The man in the bathrobe transforms into a swan.

MAN: *[pointing to the swan and talking to the bad guy woman]* So this is the big mystery? *[walking around like he owns the place]* Your husband was a swan all along?

The people having a loud conversation outside the bad guy woman's house continue to laugh, though not as loudly this time, as if they are just now tuning in and actually listening to the conversation happening inside.

BAD GUY WOMAN: I'll be good now. *[pause]* I'll tell you the truth.

The swan attempts to fly away, offstage, but the director says something and a stagehand quickly throws a net over the swan and captures it. A man from the Humane Society takes the swan away in a cage made of human bones.

MAN: Okay.

GOOD GUY WOMAN: He was never my husband.

MAN: Then what was he?

Pyramid Man discovers the home of Methuselah—Queen of the Underworld—hidden beneath the Kwik Trip, behind a dumpster. He thinks, I'd better not, and later kills himself once more by slashing his throat in a damp hotel room somewhere in Casablanca.

GOOD GUY WOMAN: I dunno really. A swan?

The laughing outside stops. Now they're definitely listening. The wall makes another sound. This time, it sounds like hands running through someone's hair.

MAN: Why did he turn into a swan? What does that mean?

One of the people outside sighs. The one woman in the

group hiccups and burps.

DRUNK WOMAN FROM OUTSIDE: *[slurring her words]* I think I'm drunk.

GOOD GUY WOMAN: *[shaking her head and looking at the now eviscerated hog sucker]* He's not my husband. This *[pointing to her chest]* is my husband.

The good guy woman pulls at a zipper above her forehead, a zipper that was hidden beneath her bangs. The zipper slides down and reveals something else, something that was hiding inside the skin of what used to be the good guy woman and that steps out.

THE THING INSIDE WHAT USED TO BE THE SKIN OF THE WOMAN WHO WAS BAD AT FIRST BUT THEN BECAME GOOD: I am the husband.

"Have You Ever Seen the Rain" by Creedence Clearwater Revival plays from some Bose speakers inside the walls of the house. There are nats of toilet paper stuck to hairs.

MAN: *[imagining thousands of caskets floating through space, the pitch-black stillness. The infinite calm, a silent escape—cosmic isolation tank]* You're the husband?

THE THING INSIDE WHAT USED TO BE THE SKIN OF THE WOMAN WHO WAS BAD AT FIRST BUT THEN BECAME GOOD: I am the husband.

MAN: *[looking at the thing inside what used to be the skin of the woman who was bad at first but then became good]* Finally, something that makes sense. *[looking at the fish on the ground]*

THE THING INSIDE WHAT USED TO BE THE SKIN OF THE WOMAN WHO WAS BAD AT FIRST BUT THEN BECAME GOOD: Yes.

MAN: So why were you pretending to be a woman this entire time?

THE THING INSIDE WHAT USED TO BE THE SKIN OF THE WOMAN WHO WAS BAD AT FIRST BUT THEN BECAME GOOD: Why did you pretend to like the fish?

MAN: What? *[looking hurt]* I actually do like the fish. *[he touches one with his foot and it explodes without sound]*

Mush and guts fly everywhere. The people having a loud conversation outside the thing inside what used to be the skin of the woman who was bad at first but then became good's house begin to leave. They throw their beer bottles against the side of the house as if they're now bored with what's been going on in the house. The wall makes the muffled sound of beer bottles breaking against the outside wall. A few bottles remain unbroken as black men appear from out of the sun, for just a few moments—and then disappear, just as quickly.

THE THING INSIDE WHAT USED TO BE THE SKIN OF THE WOMAN WHO WAS BAD AT FIRST BUT THEN BECAME GOOD: My name is Tyler.

MAN: What?

THE THING INSIDE WHAT USED TO BE THE SKIN OF THE WOMAN WHO WAS BAD AT FIRST BUT THEN BECAME GOOD: I said my name is Tyler.

MAN: *[shaking his head]* No, I think I'm going to call you Teddy. Tyler is way too hard to remember. *[pause]*

TYLER: Okay, you can call me Teddy.

MAN: Okay. *[pause]* So Teddy, why is it that you have them just lying around on the ground like that, *[pointing to the fish]* with no water or anything?

TEDDY: *[looking confused]* What's that?

Something that sounds like a tiger escapes through the wall and offstage the swan explodes like a cartoon into a million different particles of coloured paper. The net that ensconced the swan makes a quiet swoosh sound as it settles to the ground, inside the cage made of human bones.

MAN: *[looking at the particles of coloured paper]* The fish.

TEDDY: Oh. *[looking at the fish]* I guess they just don't like the water I use.

MAN: Or maybe the water doesn't like them.

TEDDY: What do you mean?

MAN: Think about it.

TEDDY: *[thinking about it]*

MAN: So hear me out. I once watched this documentary thing on PBS where the scientists were explaining that not all fish are saltwater fish. *[pause]* Right?

TEDDY: Right.

MAN: They conducted some experiments and decided that some fish actually prefer fresh water.

TEDDY: *[looking confused]* Duh.

MAN: *[to Teddy]* No, I mean, like, water we drink. *[making a motion with his arm that represents drinking water]*

TEDDY: Oh. Okay. But still, duh.

MAN: Yeah... *[pause]* Duh.

An invisible pink ray from outer space pierces the man's skull. No one can see this.

TEDDY: Yeah.

MAN: But also—I too am wearing a man suit.

The man unzips his man suit and out steps the thing inside what used to be the skin of the man who became a detective and then a man again.

THE THING INSIDE WHAT USED TO BE THE SKIN OF THE MAN WHO BECAME A DETECTIVE AND THEN A MAN AGAIN: You can call me Arthur.

TEDDY: Arthur.

ARTHUR: Teddy.

TEDDY: Arthur.

ARTHUR: *[taking off his Sherwood Forest green balaclava]* Teddy.

TEDDY: *[taking off his wild strawberry red balaclava]* Arthur.

ARTHUR: Teddy.

After a while of repeating each other's names, they kiss. As they kiss, Teddy looks over Arthur's shoulder and thinks about saying, "Duh," again. He looks at the pilot fish laying closest to him and realizes the fish's life must be very hard. The pilot fish sheds a tear, not because it feels Teddy's pain, but because it has just experienced one of the most sincere emotions of pleasure: that of knowing that from now on, it will only be given fresh water. One of the other pilot fish makes the sound of a pilot fish and Arthur cries for a bit. "Chasing Sheep is Best Left to Shepherds" by Michael Nyman plays. Teddy responds and cries even harder.

A QUASI-PHILOSOPHICAL REFLECTION ON THE MYSTERY OF THE SEVENTEEN PILOT FISH *AS PERFORMED BY TWO VERY DRUNK ADULTS*

[offstage] **WOMAN WEARING HALLOWEEN MASK MADE TO LOOK LIKE MARILYN MONROE:** I sometimes like to pretend I'm Marilyn Monroe.

[offstage] **MAN WEARING HALLOWEEN MASK MADE TO LOOK LIKE MICHAEL JACKSON:** I sometimes like to do that too, but you know she's dead, right?

[offstage] **WOMAN WEARING HALLOWEEN MASK MADE TO LOOK LIKE MARILYN MONROE:** Wait, what? *[pointing to the man wearing the Halloween mask made to look like Michael Jackson]* You also like to sometimes pretend you're Marilyn Monroe?

[offstage] **MAN WEARING HALLOWEEN MASK MADE TO LOOK LIKE MICHAEL JACKSON:** No, what I meant is that sometimes, I also like to pretend I'm someone else, like, you know, I like to put on a mask and pretend I'm someone I'm not.

Somewhere, a whale makes the sound of a whale as Galactus appears at the event horizon.

[offstage] **WOMAN WEARING HALLOWEEN MASK MADE TO LOOK LIKE MARILYN MONROE:** *[pause]* We're both sorta doing that right now.

The woman wearing the Halloween mask made to look like Marilyn Monroe hits the fast-forward button on her iPod Shuffle. The song playing makes her bob her head up and down.

[offstage] **WOMAN WEARING HALLOWEEN MASK MADE TO LOOK LIKE MARILYN MONROE:** *[pointing to face of the man wearing the Halloween mask made to look like Michael Jackson]* But you know, your mask is dead too, right?

[offstage] **MAN WEARING HALLOWEEN MASK MADE TO LOOK LIKE MICHAEL JACKSON:** *[turning the volume down on his iPod Mini because he can't hear the woman wearing the Halloween mask made to look like Marilyn Monroe]* What?

[offstage] **WOMAN WEARING HALLOWEEN MASK MADE TO LOOK LIKE MARILYN MONROE:** I said you know your mask is dead too, right?

[offstage] **MAN WEARING HALLOWEEN MASK MADE TO LOOK LIKE MICHAEL JACKSON:** *[laughing uncontrollably and pointing at his own mask]* Yeah, I know, that's what's so great about it. *[turning the volume back up on his iPod Mini]*

[offstage] **WOMAN WEARING HALLOWEEN MASK MADE TO LOOK LIKE MARILYN MONROE:** *[turning down the music on her iPod*

Shuffle and then turning her head because she couldn't hear what the man wearing the Halloween mask made to look like Michael Jackson just said]
What?

Seventeen years pass. There is a pain, but then, of course, also, there is a violence. The silence of terror in the sky comes with the groaning of the earth in oxbow. Acid rain. Rivers of blood. Tainted words. Sasquatch drowns itself. People go missing. AMBER Alerts every nine minutes— then every eight. Volcanoes disappear. Missing persons reappear. Lights in the sky emerge. Mountains materialize out of thin air, in the middle of cities, coalescing with skyscrapers and people inside the skyscrapers. Some men discover a totem in the middle of the desert. The totem is made of wood and metal and meat. A serial killer murders the superheroes of the world: Lunar Man, Sardiiiiine Person, Apples-to-Apples, Mister Magnetic, Emma Emma, Kennedy Von-Trappe, Beelzebub Mantra Kiltonyian, Apache 13, Meat & Cleaver, Africa Landscape, Tarzan, Legend of the Forest, Agatha Kristiii, Mensa Mentalis, Absolute Carnage, Augustus Maxmillian, Peter Tom Fiber Optic Traitor, Mnemo, M, Chiaroscuro Bay, Girl Drain, Open Watts, Terror Disguise, the Great Purge, Italian Forever, the Escape Plan, Pioneer Fire, Storm Setter, Chase-Maker, the Happening, Kan-Dhi, ((((o)))), Maxx Koch, the Air, the Filth, American Slap-Dash, Coin Flip, Neat-o-Mosquito, Blimp Man, Skull Hand, Tiger Flow, Opaque Road, Effervescence, Timber Girl, Approximate Solution Man, Phase 9, State of Emergency Woman, Spectacular Sequence Boy, Dave the Giant, the Priest Bishop, Open Wounds, Lazer Lazer, Migraine Man, Easy Target, Airplane Man, Savage Paper, the Cluster, the Ask, Mental Imager, Irene Lockwood, Pin Star Stripe Woman, Iraq 911, Zargon Morfoauf,

Building Boy, Mind Mantis, Texture Keeper, Asteroid Maker, the Ppppplannnnettt, Nikki Castro, Periodical Man, Mrs. Macintosh, Green Olives, the Patchwork, Impossible Now, Generic Man, Bermuda Man, Tyrant Girl, Q, Mr. Inspirational, Imp Creature, Sister Creature, Mister RepCon 35, Brother Cyst, Castle Man, Dance Dance Dance, _____, Mr. Fear, Automatic Stop, Picture Perfect, Insomniaque, Plasma Technician Boy, Theatre Sydrome, Harrier Attack, Godzilla Girl, Mr. Cancel, Comanche Man, Pistol Matt, Underground Ned, Nasty Carl, Infamous Greg, Car-Crash Samantha (and her whole squad), Prince Psycho, Lake Thing, Lo-Fi Man, Fjords Girl, Morning Air, Irish Simple, Ancestor Man, Sister Moonlight, Massive Deer Sacrifice, Fossil Boy, Crowd Girl, Environment Man (Red Version), Exotica Boy, Amazon Moon Girl, Salamander Man, Tarzan Girl v.8.3, Terminator Boy-Wonder, Song & Dance Man, Orange Moon Glow, Martian Marshall, Mayor Tomlin, Mothra Man, Toxic Maxx, Horseman, Ocarina II, Professor 5th Dimension Physics, Wall Climber, Explosion Maker, Tarp Girl, Arafat Group, Nomenclature Society Man, The New Abel & Cain, Trespass the World, Canadian Glory, the Tropics, Instant Panic Man, Peace be With You Boy, Pastor Woman, Energy Girl, Mr. Cold War, Costume Man, Fantasy Planet Kid, Yellow Cousin, Cloud Eater, Warp Rider, Basquiat Impersonator v.7.01.117b, Kinetic Fiend, Ground Hunter, Facehead, the Trilluminati Gang (Drake, Jay and Wayne), the Remover, Madame Brainwave, Ultimate Black, the Imperial Detective, Satan Divider, Metallic Green, Invisible Opaque, Skills & Violence, Twilight Man, the Final Reason, Airplane Man, the Palm Tree, High Limit, Daughter Earth, the Fascist Kiss, Emancipator 5000, Fresh Forgotten, Mr. Tomorrow, Pleasant Steve, the Brand, Extrapolation Man, 9999944259673436346221, BarcodeAnne, Tire-IronMark, Steven with the Body, Air Pressure Boy, Officer Genocide,

Frankfurt Airport Replica Man, Mz. Beautiful You, Valet Boy, Golden Paradise Girl, African Safari Man, Pitchfork Woman, Lord Altruistic, Pasadena Clarity, Melvin Macintosh, Monster Minion, Gablin Golf, Yum-Weh Pii'raate, Astro 33 Boy, Mind Bullets, Conflagrum, 3rror: Mrs. Constantinople, Brother Evans, Cloak Piece, Seventeen Layers, NASA Block, Skyhead, Oil Boy Junior, Eleven Ten, Sammy Sam Sam, Instant Machination, Tungsten Girl, Ozone Pink, Suffer Man, 99 Elements, Sig For Die, Anabelle Hemm, Rambo Incorporated, Broken Brain, Brick Face, 2 Fingers, Slam Punk, Irrevocable Man, Beneficiary Girl, Amazon Boy, 18th Century Flight Group, Sinister Valley and Appendix of the Immovable. And the serial killer, who is now able to time travel and do home invasions, also disappears—and the terror (a terror that never existed before) suddenly becomes something that is all too real.

FIN

ACKNOWLEDGMENTS

I am grateful to the following: Johnny Buse, Christian Caminiti, Conner Dylan Bassett, Emma Winsor Wood, Mario Macias, Phillip Brogdon, Justine Turnbull, Leah Dawson, Amanda Borson, Jacob Goldsmith, Jeremy Jackson, James Tadd Adcox, Trish Harnetiaux, Simon Jacobs, Ken Sparling, Christian TeBordo, Austin Breed, Tyler Crumrine, *The Grinnell Review* and my parents. Thank you all for the *moments*.

MIKE KLEINE is an American author of literary fiction. He grew up in West Africa and graduated from Grinnell College with a BA in French Literature. He currently lives somewhere in the Midwest. *The Mystery of the Seventeen Pilot Fish* is his first play.